JOURNEY TO THE
63 U.S. NATIONAL PARKS

JOURNEY TO THE
63 U.S.
NATIONAL PARKS

A JOURNAL TO PLAN, RECORD, AND REMEMBER YOUR ADVENTURES

PAIGE WUNDER

callisto
publishing
an imprint of Sourcebooks

CONTENTS

INTRODUCTION

National parks are frequently called the United States' best idea, and you're on a journey to find out exactly why. The sixty-three parks on the pages that follow have been set aside for the purpose of conservation, protection, and recreation. They contain mountains, lakes, coastlines, canyons, and so much more. Along with striking and varying landscapes, you'll find boundless adventures within each national park. Before these landscapes were governed by the National Park Service (NPS), they were roamed, cultivated, and protected by the various Indigenous tribes and cultures who called them home.

For over 150 years, people have enjoyed these parks, including the latest redesignations to national park: New River Gorge in West Virginia (2020), White Sands in New Mexico (2019), and Indiana Dunes in Indiana (2019). Even if you've previously visited a park, remember that each return can be a whole new experience based on the season, activities you try, trails you hike, or travel companions.

Whether big or small, these parks have inspired artists, writers, activists, and millions of visitors with their spectacular features. Now, you get to be moved by the beauty of them, too. The thrills you encounter, people you meet, flora and fauna you see, and unbelievable scenery that surrounds you combine to create lifelong memories.

HOW TO USE THIS BOOK

This journal and logbook will help you catalog your visits to each park. It has two sections: The first contains brief descriptions of all the U.S. national parks arranged by state, including the date each park entered NPS protection. The second is a trip log for each park in alphabetical order by state or unincorporated territory, which includes prompts for recording your memories of the parks you visit. The trip logs also include some fun facts and tips for you, including suggested photo ops. More detailed park info, such as hike descriptions, driving routes, and ranger-led activities, can be found on the NPS website (NPS.gov; see QR code below).

This journal is for you to curate your memories. It encourages you to recall things such as the date of your visit, what the weather was like, memorable moments, plant and animal life you saw, and who you were with. There's even space to sketch or get a passport stamp. There's plenty of room for you to journal about majestic scenery, favorite trails, and personal feelings or reactions, too. Plus, there are blank pages at the back of the book for any returns to previously visited parks.

Now, it's time to get out there and start exploring!

NATIONAL PARKS CHECKLIST

In every walk
with nature one
receives far more
than he seeks.

—JOHN MUIR

PLAN YOUR TRIP BEFORE YOU GO

Park Name: .... **Trip Dates:** ....

THINK ABOUT THE PARK

☐ Make reservations and apply
  for permits

☐ Check the weather ....

☐ Check for alerts, warnings, and rules ....

☐ Check the amenities and lodging ....

☐ Check the terrain and wildlife

THINK ABOUT YOUR VISIT

☐ Send your itinerary to your
  emergency contact

☐ Double check that all
  your equipment works

☐ List your goals ....

....

☐ Write down your planned activities (and a back-up plan) ....

....

THINK ABOUT YOUR ESSENTIAL SUPPLIES

☐ Extra food, water,
  and snacks

☐ Navigation tools

☐ Shelter

☐ First aid kit

☐ Extra clothing

☐ Lights, matches,
  and other tools

☐ Sun protection

ADDITIONAL SUPPLIES

....

....

....

PLAN YOUR TRIP BEFORE YOU GO

Park Name: .... **Trip Dates:** ....

THINK ABOUT THE PARK

- [ ] Make reservations and apply for permits
- [ ] Check for alerts, warnings, and rules ....
- [ ] Check the amenities and lodging ....
- [ ] Check the terrain and wildlife ....

- [ ] Check the weather ....

THINK ABOUT YOUR VISIT

- [ ] Send your itinerary to your emergency contact
- [ ] List your goals ....
....
- [ ] Write down your planned activities (and a back-up plan) ....
....

- [ ] Double check that all your equipment works

THINK ABOUT YOUR ESSENTIAL SUPPLIES

- [ ] Extra food, water, and snacks
- [ ] First aid kit

- [ ] Navigation tools
- [ ] Extra clothing
- [ ] Sun protection

- [ ] Shelter
- [ ] Lights, matches, and other tools

ADDITIONAL SUPPLIES

....
....
....

PLAN YOUR TRIP BEFORE YOU GO

Park Name: .... **Trip Dates:** ....

THINK ABOUT THE PARK

☐ Make reservations and apply for permits

☐ Check the weather ....

☐ Check for alerts, warnings, and rules ....

☐ Check the amenities and lodging ....

☐ Check the terrain and wildlife ....

THINK ABOUT YOUR VISIT

☐ Send your itinerary to your emergency contact

☐ Double check that all your equipment works

☐ List your goals ....

☐ Write down your planned activities (and a back-up plan) ....

THINK ABOUT YOUR ESSENTIAL SUPPLIES

☐ Extra food, water, and snacks

☐ Navigation tools

☐ Shelter

☐ First aid kit

☐ Extra clothing

☐ Lights, matches, and other tools

☐ Sun protection

ADDITIONAL SUPPLIES

....

....

....

PLAN YOUR TRIP BEFORE YOU GO

Park Name: ....   **Trip Dates:** ....

THINK ABOUT THE PARK

☐ Make reservations and apply for permits

☐ Check for alerts, warnings, and rules ....

☐ Check the amenities and lodging ....

☐ Check the terrain and wildlife ....

☐ Check the weather ....

THINK ABOUT YOUR VISIT

☐ Send your itinerary to your emergency contact

☐ List your goals ....

☐ Double check that all your equipment works

☐ Write down your planned activities (and a back-up plan) ....

THINK ABOUT YOUR ESSENTIAL SUPPLIES

☐ Extra food, water, and snacks

☐ First aid kit

☐ Navigation tools

☐ Extra clothing

☐ Sun protection

☐ Shelter

☐ Lights, matches, and other tools

ADDITIONAL SUPPLIES

....

....

....

PLAN YOUR TRIP BEFORE YOU GO

Park Name: _____ **Trip Dates:** _____

THINK ABOUT THE PARK

☐ Make reservations and apply for permits

☐ Check the weather _____

☐ Check for alerts, warnings, and rules _____

☐ Check the amenities and lodging _____

☐ Check the terrain and wildlife _____

THINK ABOUT YOUR VISIT

☐ Send your itinerary to your emergency contact

☐ Double check that all your equipment works

☐ List your goals _____

_____

☐ Write down your planned activities (and a back-up plan) _____

_____

THINK ABOUT YOUR ESSENTIAL SUPPLIES

☐ Extra food, water, and snacks

☐ Navigation tools

☐ Shelter

☐ First aid kit

☐ Extra clothing

☐ Lights, matches, and other tools

☐ Sun protection

ADDITIONAL SUPPLIES

_____

_____

_____

PLAN YOUR TRIP BEFORE YOU GO

Park Name: .... **Trip Dates:** ....

THINK ABOUT THE PARK

- [ ] Make reservations and apply for permits
- [ ] Check the weather ....
- [ ] Check for alerts, warnings, and rules ....
- [ ] Check the amenities and lodging
- [ ] Check the terrain and wildlife ....

THINK ABOUT YOUR VISIT

- [ ] Send your itinerary to your emergency contact
- [ ] Double check that all your equipment works
- [ ] List your goals ....

- [ ] Write down your planned activities (and a back-up plan) ....

THINK ABOUT YOUR ESSENTIAL SUPPLIES

- [ ] Extra food, water, and snacks
- [ ] Navigation tools
- [ ] Shelter
- [ ] First aid kit
- [ ] Extra clothing
- [ ] Lights, matches, and other tools
- [ ] Sun protection

ADDITIONAL SUPPLIES

....

....

....

PLAN YOUR TRIP BEFORE YOU GO

Park Name: ....   **Trip Dates:** ....

THINK ABOUT THE PARK

☐ Make reservations and apply for permits

☐ Check the weather ....

☐ Check for alerts, warnings, and rules ....

☐ Check the amenities and lodging ....

☐ Check the terrain and wildlife ....

THINK ABOUT YOUR VISIT

☐ Send your itinerary to your emergency contact

☐ Double check that all your equipment works

☐ List your goals ....

☐ Write down your planned activities (and a back-up plan) ....

THINK ABOUT YOUR ESSENTIAL SUPPLIES

☐ Extra food, water, and snacks

☐ Navigation tools

☐ Shelter

☐ First aid kit

☐ Extra clothing

☐ Sun protection

☐ Lights, matches, and other tools

ADDITIONAL SUPPLIES

....

....

....

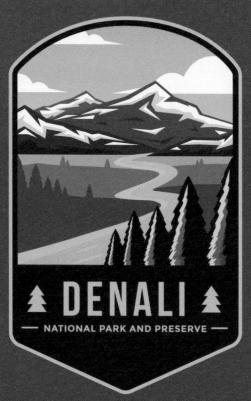

Denali National Park and Preserve

EST. FEBRUARY 1917

Containing the continent's highest mountain peak, glaciers, an abundance of wildlife, and other natural beauty, Denali is a place that you have to see to believe. This arctic tundra is a haven of raw wilderness to explore.

☐ DENALI NATIONAL PARK AND PRESERVE

Size of park: 9,492 square miles (24,584 square kilometers)

Fun fact: Glaciers cover an impressive one-sixth of Denali National Park.

Photo op: The "road to Denali" shot at mile forty-three of the park road is where you can see all of Denali Mountain on a clear day.

Date of visit: _____

Weather/Temperature: ☀ ☁ ⛅ 🌧 ❄ 🌬 🌡 🌡

Companions: _____

_____

_____

Favorite experiences: _____

_____

_____

_____

_____

_____

_____

_____

_____

_____

Notable plants and wildlife: _____

_____

_____

_____

_____

Plan to return?   Yes   No

Notes for next visit: _____

_____

_____

_____

_____

Space for sketches and/or stamps:

ALASKA

Gates of the Arctic National Park and Preserve

EST. DECEMBER 1978

Located within the Arctic Circle, this park is the definition of rugged, untouched beauty. No roads or trails exist here, and that has kept these mountains, lands, and rivers spectacularly untouched.

☐ GATES OF THE ARCTIC
NATIONAL PARK AND PRESERVE

Size of park: 13,238 square miles (34,286 square kilometers)

Fun fact: Because of its extreme remoteness, Gates of the Arctic is most often the least visited U.S. national park annually, which only adds to the excitement of making it there!

Photo op: This is one of the best places to capture a photo of the Northern Lights in all of the United States.

Date of visit: ....

Weather/Temperature: ☀ ☁ ⛅ 🌧 🌨 🌬 🌡🌡

Companions: ....

....

....

Favorite experiences: ....

....

....

....

....

....

....

ALASKA

Notable plants and wildlife: _____

_____

_____

_____

_____

Plan to return?   Yes   No

Notes for next visit: _____

_____

_____

_____

Space for sketches and/or stamps:

ALASKA

Glacier Bay National Park and Preserve

EST. FEBRUARY 1925

Turquoise-tinted glaciers collide with the ocean, creating scenic fjords and bays. Behind them, inland, are snowcapped mountains and a lush temperate rainforest filled with many trails to explore. Glacier Bay is co-managed by the Hoonah Indian Association, the tribal government of the Huna Tlingit, the tribe native to this land.

☐ GLACIER BAY NATIONAL PARK AND PRESERVE

Size of park: 5,128 square miles (13,281 square kilometers)

Fun fact: The majority of visitors to the park arrive on a cruise ship.

Photo op: Try to get a shot of the unbelievable marine wildlife, like hump-back whales or orcas, with a glacier in the background.

Date of visit: ....

Weather/Temperature: ☀ ☁ ⛅ 🌧 🌨 💨 🌡🌡

Companions: ....

....

....

Favorite experiences: ....

....

....

....

....

....

....

....

....

ALASKA

Notable plants and wildlife:

Plan to return?   Yes   No

Notes for next visit:

Space for sketches and/or stamps:

Katmai National Park and Preserve

EST. SEPTEMBER 1918

Although notorious for its large brown bear
population, the park's land itself is remarkable.
This wild park has tons of backcountry
opportunities through coastline, mountains,
multiple volcanoes, valleys, and so much more.

☐ KATMAI NATIONAL PARK AND PRESERVE

Size of park: 6,396 square miles (16,566 square kilometers)

Fun fact: There are at least fourteen different volcanoes in the park boundary.

Photo op: Don't miss the famous waterfall filled with bears at Brooks Camp.

Date of visit: ....

Weather/Temperature: ☀ ☁ ⛅ 🌧 🌨 🌬 🌡 🌡

Companions: ....

....

....

Favorite experiences: ....

....

....

....

....

....

....

....

....

Notable plants and wildlife: _____

_____

_____

_____

_____

Plan to return?   Yes   No

Notes for next visit: _____

_____

_____

_____

_____

Space for sketches and/or stamps:

Kenai Fjords National Park

EST. DECEMBER 1978

This glacial dreamland is unlike anything else you'll see in the United States. From coastal fjords containing calving glaciers to hiking trails leading up and over glaciers, prepare to be awed.

☐ KENAI FJORDS NATIONAL PARK

Size of park: 1,046 square miles (2,709 square kilometers)

Fun fact: About half of the land in this park is covered by glaciers.

Photo op: Get out on the water and capture the beauty of the fjords and the wildlife, sea stacks, and glaciers within them.

Date of visit: ....

Weather/Temperature: ☀ ☁ ⛅ 🌧 🌨 💨 🌡🌡

Companions: ....

....

....

Favorite experiences: ....

....

....

....

....

....

....

....

....

ALASKA

Notable plants and wildlife: _____
_____
_____
_____
_____

Plan to return?   Yes   No

Notes for next visit: _____
_____
_____
_____
_____

Space for sketches and/or stamps:

ALASKA

Kobuk Valley National Park

EST. DECEMBER 1978

Annually, 500,000 caribou migrate here, and many other species call it home. Additionally, this park boasts mountains, forests, and a massive concentration of high-latitude sand dunes.

☐ KOBUK VALLEY NATIONAL PARK

Size of park: 2,735 square miles (7,084 square kilometers)

Fun fact: Even though it's entirely in the Arctic Circle, temps on top of the sand dunes can reach 100-plus degrees in the summer.

Photo op: Take a photo on top of the Great Kobuk Sand Dunes. People will never believe that the photo was taken in Alaska.

Date of visit: ....

Weather/Temperature: ☀ ☁ ⛅ 🌧 🌨 💨 🌡 🌡

Companions: ....

....

....

Favorite experiences: ....

....

....

....

....

....

....

....

....

ALASKA

Notable plants and wildlife: _____

_____

_____

_____

_____

Plan to return?   Yes   No

Notes for next visit: _____

_____

_____

_____

_____

Space for sketches and/or stamps:

ALASKA

Lake Clark National Park and Preserve

EST. DECEMBER 1978

Rocky, snowcapped mountains and steaming volcanoes create the backdrop for this park. Accented by turquoise lakes and lush valleys, it's perfect for outdoor enthusiasts of all kinds.

☐ LAKE CLARK NATIONAL PARK AND PRESERVE

Size of park: 6,297 square miles (16,309 square kilometers)

Fun fact: There's only one known amphibian in this park, the wood frog.

Photo op: Take the perfect reflection shot of the mountains behind Lake Clark.

Date of visit: ....

Weather/Temperature: ☀ ☁ 🌤 🌧 🌨 🌬 🌡 🌡

Companions: ....

....

....

Favorite experiences: ....

....

....

....

....

....

....

....

....

Notable plants and wildlife:

_____

_____

_____

_____

_____

Plan to return?   Yes   No

Notes for next visit:

_____

_____

_____

_____

_____

Space for sketches and/or stamps:

ALASKA

WRANGELL-ST. ELIAS

NATIONAL PARK
AND PRESERVE

Wrangell-St. Elias National
Park and Preserve

EST. DECEMBER 1978

This is the largest national park (roughly the size of Belgium, Slovenia, and Luxembourg combined), and it has big, big beauty! There are glaciers, ice caves, volcanoes, massive mountains, gorgeous boreal forests, and loads of wildlife.

☐ WRANGELL-ST. ELIAS
NATIONAL PARK AND PRESERVE

Size of park: 20,587 square miles (53,320 square kilometers)

Fun fact: This park has the second highest elevation of the U.S. national parks at 18,008 feet, and it goes all the way down to sea level.

Photo op: Capture the gorgeous mountains towering beyond the Kuskulana Bridge for that perfect adventure road trip shot.

Date of visit: ....

Weather/Temperature: ☀ ☁ ⛅ 🌧 🌨 🌬 🌡 🌡

Companions: ....

....

....

Favorite experiences: ....

....

....

....

....

....

....

....

Notable plants and wildlife: ....
....
....
....
....

Plan to return?   Yes   No

Notes for next visit: ....
....
....
....
....

Space for sketches and/or stamps:

NATIONAL PARK OF
AMERICAN SAMOA

National Park of American Samoa

EST. OCTOBER 1988

This tropical park located in the South Pacific is home to cultural sites, bright blue waters, and interesting wildlife, like fruit bats! Popular activities here are snorkeling over coral reefs and hiking.

☐ NATIONAL PARK OF AMERICAN SAMOA

Size of park: 13 square miles (34 square kilometers)

Fun fact: This is the only U.S. national park located south of the equator.

Photo op: The Tuafanua Trail offers some of the most beautiful coastline viewpoints, perfect for photographing.

Date of visit: ....

Weather/Temperature: ☀ ⛅ 🌤 🌧 🌨 🌬 🌡

Companions: ....

....

....

Favorite experiences: ....

....

....

....

....

....

....

....

....

Notable plants and wildlife: _____

_____

_____

_____

_____

Plan to return?   Yes   No

Notes for next visit: _____

_____

_____

_____

_____

Space for sketches and/or stamps:

Grand Canyon National Park

EST. FEBRUARY 1919

Home of the Grand Canyon, this park was carved by the Colorado River. Layers of different shades of pink, brown, and red stone make up the walls that reach a depth of up to a mile. This is a place filled with wonder.

☐ GRAND CANYON NATIONAL PARK

Size of park: 1,878 square miles (4,864 square kilometers)

Fun fact: Although the North and South Rims belong to the same canyon, the experiences are drastically different. The North Rim is tree covered, less crowded, and cooler. The South Rim is more of what you picture: more popular and much hotter!

Photo op: Hopi Point has a spectacular view of this massive canyon that's extra stellar at sunrise or sunset.

Date of visit: ....

Weather/Temperature: ☀ ☁ ⛅ 🌧 ❄ 🌬 🌡🌡

Companions: ....

....

....

Favorite experiences: ....

....

....

....

....

....

....

....

....

ARIZONA

Notable plants and wildlife: ....

....

....

....

....

Plan to return?   Yes   No

Notes for next visit: ....

....

....

....

....

Space for sketches and/or stamps:

ARIZONA

Petrified Forest National Park

EST. DECEMBER 1906

This park boasts an incredible collection of fossilized trees from the Triassic period, along with other impressive fossils. Petrified Forest is divided between desert and prairie with gorgeous formations and badlands dispersed throughout.

☐ PETRIFIED FOREST NATIONAL PARK

Size of park: 346 square miles (896 square kilometers)

Fun fact: Historic Route 66 cuts right through the national park.

Photo op: Be sure to snap a photo of the Blue Mesa badlands, either from the overlook above or down in the midst of them.

Date of visit: _____

Weather/Temperature: ☀ ☁ ⛅ 🌧 🌨 💨 🌡 🌡

Companions: _____

_____

_____

Favorite experiences: _____

_____

_____

_____

_____

_____

_____

_____

_____

ARIZONA

Notable plants and wildlife:

_____

_____

_____

_____

Plan to return?   Yes   No

Notes for next visit: _____

_____

_____

_____

_____

Space for sketches and/or stamps:

Saguaro National Park

EST. MARCH 1933

Saguaro protects the largest species of cactus in the United States, the iconic cacti that easily average forty feet tall. You'll see thousands of saguaros surrounded by mountains and other desert formations. Don't skip the sunset views here.

☐ SAGUARO NATIONAL PARK

Size of park: 145 square miles (376 square kilometers)

Fun fact: Saguaro cacti typically live between 150 and 175 years.

Photo op: Take a sunset photo filled with saguaros along Ajo Mountain Drive.

Date of visit: ....

Weather/Temperature: ☀ ☁ ⛅ 🌧 🌨 💨 🌡 🌡

Companions: ....

....

....

Favorite experiences: ....

....

....

....

....

....

....

....

Notable plants and wildlife: _____

_____

_____

_____

_____

Plan to return?   Yes   No

Notes for next visit: _____

_____

_____

_____

_____

Space for sketches and/or stamps:

Hot Springs National Park

EST. APRIL 1832

Nestled in the Ouachita Mountains,
this park protects the forests, the hills,
and the thermal hot springs, as well as
Bathhouse Row in town, where you
can soak in the healing waters.

☐ HOT SPRINGS NATIONAL PARK

Size of park: 9 square miles (23 square kilometers)

Fun fact: The hot springs here aren't caused by volcanic activity. Instead, they're due to a phenomenon called "geothermal gradient."

Photo op: Snap a pic of the beautiful buildings that make up Bathhouse Row.

Date of visit: _____

Weather/Temperature: ☀️ ☁️ ⛅ 🌧️ 🌨️ 🌬️ 🌡️🌡️

Companions: _____

_____

_____

Favorite experiences: _____

_____

_____

_____

_____

_____

_____

_____

ARKANSAS

Notable plants and wildlife: _____

_____

_____

_____

_____

Plan to return?   Yes   No

Notes for next visit: _____

_____

_____

_____

_____

Space for sketches and/or stamps:

Channel Islands National Park

EST. APRIL 1938

Five islands off the coast of California make up this cornucopia of wildlife and plants, some of which are endemic. Plus, the stunning rocky island landscape and bright blue waters will leave you awestruck.

☐ CHANNEL ISLANDS NATIONAL PARK

Size of park: 390 square miles (1,010 square kilometers)

Fun fact: Nearly 150 species of animals are endemic to these islands, giving this park its nickname, "North America's Galapagos."

Photo op: Don't miss the stunning Inspiration Point, which overlooks smaller islands and blue waters on the East Anacapa Island Trail.

Date of visit:

Weather/Temperature:

Companions:

Favorite experiences:

Notable plants and wildlife: _____

_____

_____

_____

_____

Plan to return?   Yes   No

Notes for next visit: _____

_____

_____

_____

Space for sketches and/or stamps:

Death Valley National Park

EST. FEBRUARY 1933

Death Valley is a land of extremes: It's the lowest point in North America, with the hottest temps ever recorded. Expect rugged landscapes next to smooth sand dunes, a volcanic crater, multicolored mountains, and more!

☐ DEATH VALLEY NATIONAL PARK

Size of park: 5,326 square miles (13,794 square kilometers)

Fun fact: Death Valley is the largest national park in the Lower 48 states.

Photo op: Artists Palette is the perfect place to snap a photo of one of the park's most unique formations—a brightly colored mountainside. Colors are best in the evening.

Date of visit: _____

Weather/Temperature: ☀ ☁ ⛅ 🌧 🌨 🌬 🌡 🌡

Companions: _____

_____

_____

Favorite experiences: _____

_____

_____

_____

_____

_____

_____

Notable plants and wildlife: _____

_____

_____

_____

_____

Plan to return?   Yes   No

Notes for next visit: _____

_____

_____

_____

_____

Space for sketches and/or stamps:

Joshua Tree National Park

EST. AUGUST 1936

This desert landscape is filled with formations, flora, and fauna, including the distinctive Joshua trees that give the park its name. This park is famous for its climbing and hiking opportunities.

☐ JOSHUA TREE NATIONAL PARK

Size of park: 1,242 square miles (3,218 square kilometers)

Fun fact: Joshua trees aren't trees at all. They're actually a type of yucca.

Photo op: Don't miss the sunset at the Cholla Cactus Garden for a super-interesting photo.

Date of visit: ....

Weather/Temperature: ☀ ☁ ⛅ 🌧 🌨 💨 🌡 🌡

Companions: ....

....

....

Favorite experiences: ....

....

....

....

....

....

....

....

....

Notable plants and wildlife: _____

_____

_____

_____

_____

Plan to return?   Yes   No

Notes for next visit: _____

_____

_____

_____

_____

Space for sketches and/or stamps:

Kings Canyon National Park

EST. OCTOBER 1890

You can explore the wondrous Sierra Nevada
mountain range without the crowds of other parks.
These massive mountains, deep valleys, and forests
have so much beauty to marvel at. This park borders
Sequoia National Park, so don't miss visiting it.

☐ KINGS CANYON NATIONAL PARK

Size of park: 722 square miles (1,869 square kilometers)

Fun fact: Kings Canyon, which was carved by glaciers, is actually deeper than the Grand Canyon.

Photo op: Snap that quintessential High Sierra shot from the Mist Falls Trail. The waterfall is an added bonus, but the mountain views are the highlight.

Date of visit: ....

Weather/Temperature: ☀ ☁ ⛅ 🌧 🌨 💨 🌡 🌡

Companions: ....

....

....

Favorite experiences: ....

....

....

....

....

....

....

....

....

Notable plants and wildlife: ....

....

....

....

....

Plan to return?   Yes   No

Notes for next visit: ....

....

....

....

....

Space for sketches and/or stamps:

Lassen Volcanic National Park

EST. MAY 1907

This park houses all four types of volcanoes, including the world's largest plug dome volcano. Mountains of the Cascade Range, bubbling mud pots, steaming fumaroles, and pristine lakes create distinct beauty here.

☐ LASSEN VOLCANIC NATIONAL PARK

Size of park: 167 square miles (433 square kilometers)

Fun fact: All four types of volcanoes (cinder cone, composite, plug dome, and shield) can be found within this one national park.

Photo op: Don't miss the view of Lassen Peak towering over the stunning alpine lake, Lake Helen.

Date of visit: ....

Weather/Temperature: ☀ ☁ ⛅ 🌧 🌨 💨 🌡 🌡

Companions: ....

....

....

Favorite experiences: ....

....

....

....

....

....

....

....

CALIFORNIA

Notable plants and wildlife: _____
_____
_____
_____
_____

Plan to return?   Yes   No

Notes for next visit: _____
_____
_____
_____
_____

Space for sketches and/or stamps:

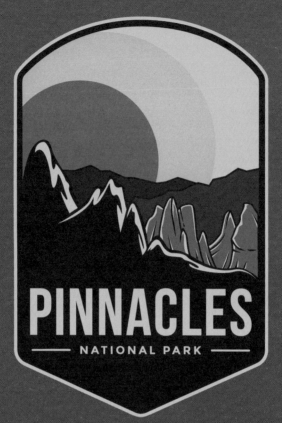

Pinnacles National Park

EST. JANUARY 1908

Pinnacles is famous for a concentrated collection of jagged rock pillars rising from the ground. They were formed by major volcanic activity. Alongside the Pinnacles are canyons, springs, and caves.

☐ PINNACLES NATIONAL PARK

Size of park: 42 square miles (109 square kilometers)

Fun fact: Just under 500 bee species live in Pinnacles National Park, making Pinnacles one of the most bee-diverse places on earth.

Photo op: High Peaks Trail offers some of the most spectacular opportunities to look down over the rock formations.

Date of visit: _____

Weather/Temperature: ☀ ☁ ⛅ 🌧 🌨 💨 🌡🌡

Companions: _____

_____

_____

Favorite experiences: _____

_____

_____

_____

_____

_____

_____

_____

_____

CALIFORNIA

Notable plants and wildlife:

Plan to return?   Yes   No

Notes for next visit:

Space for sketches and/or stamps:

CALIFORNIA

Redwood National and State Parks

EST. OCTOBER 1968

These rainforest parks are filled with ferns, wildflowers, and, most notably, redwood trees. Although the forests get all the glory, there are also miles of coastlines, rivers, and lush canyons protected here.

☐ REDWOOD NATIONAL AND STATE PARKS

Size of park: 217 square miles (562 square kilometers)

Fun fact: Although three different species of redwood trees exist, the coast redwood is the only one you can find in this national park.

Photo op: Lady Bird Johnson Grove Trail offers up some amazing views of towering redwood trees.

Date of visit: ....

Weather/Temperature: ☀️ ⛅ 🌤️ 🌧️ 🌨️ 🌬️ 🌡️

Companions: ....

....

....

Favorite experiences: ....

....

....

....

....

....

....

....

Notable plants and wildlife:

_____

_____

_____

_____

Plan to return?   Yes   No

Notes for next visit: _____

_____

_____

_____

Space for sketches and/or stamps:

Sequoia National Park

EST. SEPTEMBER 1890

This Sierra Nevada–based park is one where the mountains aren't the biggest draw; it's all about the sequoias. These ancient, massive trees fill groves here, including the world's largest tree (by volume), General Sherman, which sits at 275 feet tall and 36 feet in diameter at the base. This park borders Kings Canyon National Park, so don't miss visiting it.

☐ SEQUOIA NATIONAL PARK

Size of park: 631 square miles (1,634 square kilometers)

Fun fact: Fire actually plays a role in the survival of sequoias. Low-intensity fires are needed to make the cones from giant sequoias open up.

Photo op: Moro Rock's peak offers the best spot to take a jaw-dropping photo in the park.

Date of visit: ....

Weather/Temperature: ☀ ⛅ 🌤 🌧 ❄ 💨 🌡🌡

Companions: ....

....

....

Favorite experiences: ....

....

....

....

....

....

....

....

....

Notable plants and wildlife: _____

_____

_____

_____

_____

Plan to return?   Yes   No

Notes for next visit: _____

_____

_____

_____

_____

Space for sketches and/or stamps:

Yosemite National Park

EST. OCTOBER 1890

Mountains of all shapes rise up over glacier-carved valleys where world-renowned climbers congregate. Trails lead to massive waterfalls, through ancient forests and fields of wildflowers. Its beauty is almost unbelievable.

☐ YOSEMITE NATIONAL PARK

Size of park: 1,190 square miles (3,082 square kilometers)

Fun fact: Legendary writer and naturalist John Muir was instrumental in the creation and later expansion of Yosemite National Park. His famous quote, "The mountains are calling and I must go," refers to the mountains of Yosemite.

Photo op: Glacier Point is the perfect place to photograph Half Dome. When the roads are open, you can drive there. When the road is closed, you can access it via a few trails, the shortest of which is Four Mile Trail, which is 9.6 miles round trip.

Date of visit: ....

Weather/Temperature: ☀ ☁ ⛅ 🌧 ❄ 🌬 🌡 🌡

Companions: ....

....

....

Favorite experiences: ....

....

....

....

....

....

Notable plants and wildlife: ....
....
....
....
....

Plan to return?   Yes   No

Notes for next visit: ....
....
....
....
....

Space for sketches and/or stamps:

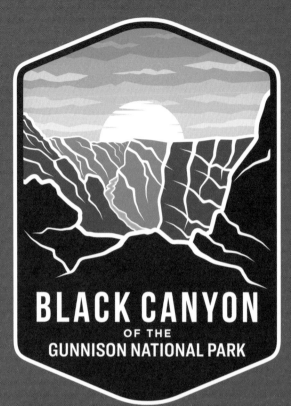

Black Canyon of the Gunnison National Park

EST. MARCH 1933

This canyon's narrow opening makes it incredibly steep and very rugged, with jaw-dropping views all the way down to the Gunnison River. Adventurers, this park is for you.

☐ BLACK CANYON OF THE GUNNISON NATIONAL PARK

Size of park: 48 square miles (124 square kilometers)

Fun fact: Black Canyon's Painted Wall is taller than many of the tallest skyscrapers, including Chicago's Willis Tower.

Photo op: The view of Painted Wall from Chasm View Nature Trail is spectacular.

Date of visit: _____

Weather/Temperature: ☀ ☁ ⛅ 🌧 🌨 🌬 🌡 🌡

Companions: _____

_____

_____

Favorite experiences: _____

_____

_____

_____

_____

_____

_____

COLORADO

Notable plants and wildlife: _____

_____

_____

_____

_____

Plan to return?   Yes   No

Notes for next visit: _____

_____

_____

_____

_____

Space for sketches and/or stamps:

COLORADO

Great Sand Dunes National Park and Preserve

EST. MARCH 1932

Sliding down the continent's tallest dunes is probably the most common activity here. However, don't miss seeing the mountains, forests, and alpine lakes the park also has to offer.

☐ GREAT SAND DUNES
NATIONAL PARK AND PRESERVE

Size of park: 233 square miles (603 square kilometers)

Fun fact: You can hear sand "sing" here, when grains of sand fall. This is heard most loudly during avalanches.

Photo op: Snap a pic from one of the tallest dunes (High, Star, or Hidden Dunes), looking down over the others that surround them.

Date of visit: ....

Weather/Temperature: ☀ ☁ ⛅ 🌧 ❄ 💨 🌡 🌡

Companions: ....

....

....

Favorite experiences: ....

....

....

....

....

....

....

COLORADO

Notable plants and wildlife: _____

_____

_____

_____

_____

Plan to return?   Yes   No

Notes for next visit: _____

_____

_____

_____

_____

Space for sketches and/or stamps:

Mesa Verde National Park

EST. JUNE 1906

Mesa Verde houses one of the most impressive and vast collections of Puebloan cliff dwellings tucked into the overhang of the mesa. Trails lead in and around the dwellings, as well as into the surrounding scenic parklands.

☐ MESA VERDE NATIONAL PARK

Size of park: 82 square miles (212 square kilometers)

Fun fact: There are over 600 cliff dwellings in this national park.

Photo op: Snap the iconic Mesa Verde dwelling photo from the Spruce Tree House Trail for the perfect overlook.

Date of visit: _____

Weather/Temperature: ☀ ☁ ⛅ 🌧 🌨 💨 🌡 🌡

Companions: _____

_____

_____

Favorite experiences: _____

_____

_____

_____

_____

_____

_____

_____

_____

Notable plants and wildlife: _____

_____

_____

_____

_____

Plan to return?   Yes   No

Notes for next visit: _____

_____

_____

_____

_____

Space for sketches and/or stamps:

COLORADO

Rocky Mountain National Park

EST. JANUARY 1915

The Rockies tower over sparkling alpine lakes, glacial-carved meadows tucked in valleys filled with stunning seasonal wildflowers, and waterfalls that flow down the mountainsides. This park has no shortage of beauty.

☐ ROCKY MOUNTAIN NATIONAL PARK

Size of park: 415 square miles (1,075 square kilometers)

Fun fact: There are sixty peaks in the park that tower 12,000 feet or higher.

Photo op: Snap a photo of Emerald Lake, the alpine lake with a mountain backdrop. It's worth the hike.

Date of visit:

Weather/Temperature:

Companions:

Favorite experiences:

Notable plants and wildlife: _____

_____

_____

_____

_____

Plan to return?   Yes   No

Notes for next visit: _____

_____

_____

_____

_____

Space for sketches and/or stamps:

COLORADO

Biscayne National Park

EST. OCTOBER 1968

This coastal park is most famous for the beauty that lies below the surface of the ocean. Coral reefs, a wide variety of wildlife, and even shipwrecks are waiting to be explored here.

☐ BISCAYNE NATIONAL PARK

Size of park: 270 square miles (699 square kilometers)

Fun fact: Biscayne is home to four completely different ecosystems.

Photo op: Boca Chita Key Lighthouse overlooking the teal waters is the perfect place to snap a photo.

Date of visit: ....

Weather/Temperature: ☀️ ☁️ 🌤️ 🌧️ 🌨️ 💨 🌡️🌡️

Companions: ....

....

....

Favorite experiences: ....

....

....

....

....

....

....

....

....

Notable plants and wildlife: _____

_____

_____

_____

_____

Plan to return?   Yes   No

Notes for next visit: _____

_____

_____

_____

_____

Space for sketches and/or stamps:

Dry Tortugas National Park

EST. JANUARY 1935

Although this park houses coastal fortress Fort Jefferson, the show-stealer is the teal-blue water surrounding the seven protected islands and all the incredible wildlife that dwells here. An astonishing 99 percent of this park is underwater.

☐ DRY TORTUGAS NATIONAL PARK

Size of park: 101 square miles (262 square kilometers)

Fun fact: There are hundreds of shipwrecks resting on the ocean floor in the waters surrounding Dry Tortugas.

Photo op: Check out Fort Jefferson's manmade beauty with the teal waters in the background.

Date of visit: ....

Weather/Temperature: ☀️ ☁️ ⛅ 🌧️ 🌨️ 💨 🌡️🌡️

Companions: ....

....

....

Favorite experiences: ....

....

....

....

....

....

....

....

Notable plants and wildlife:

_____

_____

_____

_____

_____

Plan to return?   Yes   No

Notes for next visit: _____

_____

_____

_____

_____

Space for sketches and/or stamps:

Everglades National Park

EST. MAY 1934

This subtropical, mostly wetlands park is home to wild beauty and many unique animals, such as Florida panthers, manatees, and crocodiles. Getting out in the marshy waters is the best way to spot wildlife and explore the park.

☐ EVERGLADES NATIONAL PARK

Size of park: 2,358 square miles (6,107 square kilometers)

Fun fact: This is the only place in the world where alligators and crocodiles coexist.

Photo op: Snap pics of as many of the famous park animals as you can find from the boardwalk on the Anhinga Trail.

Date of visit: _____

Weather/Temperature: ☀ ☁ ⛅ 🌧 🌨 🌬 🌡 🌡

Companions: _____

_____

_____

Favorite experiences: _____

_____

_____

_____

_____

_____

_____

_____

_____

Notable plants and wildlife: _____
_____
_____
_____
_____

Plan to return?   Yes   No

Notes for next visit: _____
_____
_____
_____
_____

Space for sketches and/or stamps:

FLORIDA

Haleakalā National Park

EST. AUGUST 1916

This striking park has it all: coastlines, waterfalls, rainforest, hills, and a very large, dormant volcano. The most notable thing to do here is catch the sunrise from above the clouds.

☐ HALEAKALĀ NATIONAL PARK

Size of park: 52 square miles (135 square kilometers)

Fun fact: This park is more than just the Haleakalā area. There's a section full of lush rainforest, coastal views, and waterfalls.

Photo op: The sunrise from above the clouds atop Haleakalā Crater is one of the most spectacular sunrises you'll ever see.

Date of visit: _____

Weather/Temperature: ☀ ☁ ⛅ 🌧 🌨 💨 🌡🌡

Companions: _____

_____

_____

Favorite experiences: _____

_____

_____

_____

_____

_____

_____

_____

HAWAI'I

Notable plants and wildlife: ....
....
....
....
....

Plan to return?   Yes   No

Notes for next visit: ....
....
....
....

Space for sketches and/or stamps:

Hawai'i Volcanoes National Park

EST. AUGUST 1916

The two volcanoes that give this park its name are active and changing the island of Hawai'i. This park celebrates and protects the changes they've created, such as craters, lava tubes, and sea arches.

☐ HAWAI'I VOLCANOES NATIONAL PARK

Size of park: 513 square miles (1,329 square kilometers)

Fun fact: This park is home to the largest active volcano in the entire world, Mauna Loa.

Photo op: Try to safely find some lava to photograph. Ask a park ranger for the best spot to watch the island change before your eyes.

Date of visit: _____

Weather/Temperature: ☀ ☁ ⛅ 🌧 ❄ 🌬 🌡 🌡

Companions: _____

_____

Favorite experiences: _____

_____

_____

_____

_____

_____

_____

HAWAI'I

Notable plants and wildlife:

Plan to return?   Yes   No

Notes for next visit:

Space for sketches and/or stamps:

Indiana Dunes National Park

EST. NOVEMBER 1966

These dunes rest against the shores of Lake Michigan. Lakefront beaches here are perfect for relaxing. Also, there are trails through the surrounding forest and even over the dunes themselves.

☐ INDIANA DUNES NATIONAL PARK

Size of park: 24 square miles (62 square kilometers)

Fun fact: This national park has more native species of orchids than the entire state of Hawai'i!

Photo op: Get that perfect shot down the boardwalk of Dune Succession Trail.

Date of visit: ....

Weather/Temperature: ☀ ☁ ⛅ 🌧 ❄ 🌬 🌡 🌡

Companions: ....

....

....

Favorite experiences: ....

....

....

....

....

....

....

....

INDIANA

Notable plants and wildlife:

_____

_____

_____

_____

Plan to return?   Yes   No

Notes for next visit: _____

_____

_____

_____

_____

Space for sketches and/or stamps:

Mammoth Cave National Park

EST. MAY 1926

Mammoth perfectly describes the world's longest cave system. Currently, thirteen different cave tours take you into them, showing off formations and history. Aboveground, day use and backcountry trails wind through the woods.

☐ MAMMOTH CAVE NATIONAL PARK

Size of park: 84 square miles (218 square kilometers)

Fun fact: Mammoth Cave is home to Kentucky cave shrimp, which are not only endemic to the park but also found only in this one cave.

Photo op: Capture a photo of Frozen Niagara, a beautiful formation found inside Mammoth Cave.

Date of visit: _____

Weather/Temperature: ☀ ☁ ⛅ 🌧 ❄ 🌬 🌡 🌡

Companions: _____

_____

_____

Favorite experiences: _____

_____

_____

_____

_____

_____

_____

_____

Notable plants and wildlife: ....

....

....

....

....

Plan to return?   Yes   No

Notes for next visit: ....

....

....

....

....

Space for sketches and/or stamps:

KENTUCKY

Acadia National Park

EST. JULY 1916

Acadia is home to more than sixty miles of high, rocky, rugged Atlantic coastline. Trails up granite mountains, like the famous Cadillac Mountain, offer mountain and coastal views.

☐ ACADIA NATIONAL PARK

Size of park: 77 square miles (199 square kilometers)

Fun fact: For part of the year, Acadia is the place to see the first sight of the sunrise in the United States.

Photo op: Bass Harbor Head Light Station is commonly shot with the rugged coastline in the foreground.

Date of visit: ....

Weather/Temperature: ☀ ☁ 🌤 🌧 🌨 💨 🌡 🌡

Companions: ....

....

....

Favorite experiences: ....

....

....

....

....

....

....

....

....

MAINE

Notable plants and wildlife: _____
_____
_____
_____
_____

Plan to return?   Yes   No

Notes for next visit: _____
_____
_____
_____

Space for sketches and/or stamps:

MAINE

Isle Royale National Park

EST. MARCH 1931

This park is made up of a remote archipelago on Lake Superior. The car-free islands contain stunning forests and rugged lakefront to explore by boat and on foot.

☐ ISLE ROYALE NATIONAL PARK

Size of park: 893 square miles (2,313 square kilometers)

Fun fact: This park is home to the longest-running ecological study on a mammal predator-prey system in the world, which is the gray wolf and moose.

Photo op: You'll want to capture the view from Scoville Point; it's a stunner.

Date of visit: _____

Weather/Temperature: ☀ ☁ ⛅ 🌧 ❄ 🌬 🌡🌡

Companions: _____

_____

_____

Favorite experiences: _____

_____

_____

_____

_____

_____

_____

Notable plants and wildlife:

_____

_____

_____

_____

_____

Plan to return?   Yes   No

Notes for next visit: _____

_____

_____

_____

_____

Space for sketches and/or stamps:

MICHIGAN

Voyageurs National Park

EST. JANUARY 1971

Voyageurs protects lakes, lakeshores, and forests, all of which feel very untouched. Many animals, such as moose and wolves, call this park home, and it's a great place to catch the Northern Lights.

☐ VOYAGEURS NATIONAL PARK

Size of park: 341 square miles (883 square kilometers)

Fun fact: Voyageurs is home to some of the oldest rock formations in the entire world—some are up to 2.8 billion years old and are from the creation of the continent.

Photo op: The stunning view at Kabetogama Lake Overlook makes a perfect photo.

Date of visit: ....

Weather/Temperature: ☀ ☁ ⛅ 🌧 🌨 💨 🌡 🌡

Companions: ....

....

....

Favorite experiences: ....

....

....

....

....

....

....

....

MINNESOTA

Notable plants and wildlife: _____

_____

_____

_____

_____

Plan to return?   Yes   No

Notes for next visit: _____

_____

_____

_____

_____

Space for sketches and/or stamps:

MINNESOTA

Gateway Arch National Park

EST. DECEMBER 1935

Located completely within St. Louis, this park celebrates the area where Lewis and Clark set out on their journey west, Dred Scott had his famous fight for freedom, and the Gateway Arch is located.

☐ GATEWAY ARCH NATIONAL PARK

Size of park: 0.30 square miles (0.78 square kilometers)

Fun fact: The Gateway Arch is the world's tallest arch and is just as wide as it is tall!

Photo op: Snag the two famous views of the park: looking up at the arch and the view from the top of the arch.

Date of visit: _____

Weather/Temperature: ☀️ ☁️ ⛅ 🌧️ 🌨️ 🌬️ 🌡️ 🌡️

Companions: _____

_____

_____

Favorite experiences: _____

_____

_____

_____

_____

_____

_____

_____

MISSOURI

Notable plants and wildlife: _____

_____

_____

_____

_____

Plan to return?   Yes   No

Notes for next visit: _____

_____

_____

_____

_____

Space for sketches and/or stamps:

MISSOURI

Glacier National Park

EST. MAY 1910

Millions of years in the making, glaciers carved out the beautiful landscapes we see today. These teal lakes, mountains, hanging valleys, and waterfalls create some of the United States' most stunning scenes.

☐ GLACIER NATIONAL PARK

Size of park: 1,583 square miles (4,100 square kilometers)

Fun fact: One of the park's peaks, Triple Divide Peak, supplies water to three different oceans: the Atlantic, Pacific, and Arctic Oceans.

Photo op: Hidden Lake Overlook is an awe-inspiring landscape you'll be glad you photographed.

Date of visit:

Weather/Temperature: ☀ ☁ ⛅ 🌧 ❄ 🌬 🌡 🌡

Companions:

Favorite experiences:

MONTANA

Notable plants and wildlife: _____
_____
_____
_____
_____

Plan to return?   Yes   No

Notes for next visit: _____
_____
_____
_____
_____

Space for sketches and/or stamps:

Great Basin National Park

EST. JANUARY 1922

A showstopper above and below the ground, this park boasts a wide array of natural sites: caves, mountains, a large concentration of bristlecone pines, and even a glacier.

☐ GREAT BASIN NATIONAL PARK

Size of park: 121 square miles (313 square kilometers)

Fun fact: The bristlecone pines here are some of the oldest trees in the world.

Photo op: Capture the turquoise waters of Teresa Lake with the mountains rising up behind.

Date of visit: _____

Weather/Temperature: ☀ ☁ 🌤 🌧 🌨 🌬 🌡🌡

Companions: _____

_____

_____

Favorite experiences: _____

_____

_____

_____

_____

_____

_____

_____

Notable plants and wildlife:

Plan to return?   Yes   No

Notes for next visit:

Space for sketches and/or stamps:

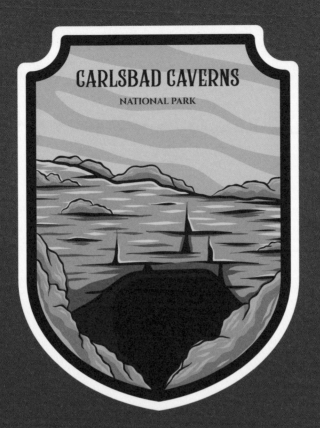

Carlsbad Caverns National Park

EST. OCTOBER 1923

This park is known for its expansive cave system, filled with otherworldly ornate stalactites, stalagmites, and pools throughout the 100-plus caves. The desert landscape aboveground is also worth exploring.

☐ CARLSBAD CAVERNS NATIONAL PARK

Size of park: 73 square miles (189 square kilometers)

Fun fact: Carlsbad's caverns were formed by sulfuric acid, unlike most lime-stone caves, which are typically formed by water.

Photo op: The Big Room inside Carlsbad Caverns shows the massive scale of these caves.

Date of visit: ....

Weather/Temperature: ☀ ☁ ⛅ 🌧 🌨 🌬 🌡 🌡

Companions: ....

....

....

Favorite experiences: ....

....

....

....

....

....

....

....

NEW MEXICO

Notable plants and wildlife:

_____

_____

_____

_____

Plan to return?   Yes   No

Notes for next visit: _____

_____

_____

_____

Space for sketches and/or stamps:

White Sands National Park

EST. JANUARY 1933

Gypsum crystals created the iconic white sands that make up the dunes here. Although they're not the tallest dunes, they're still gorgeous and impressive to drive through, hike over, and slide down.

☐ WHITE SANDS NATIONAL PARK

Size of park: 229 square miles (593 square kilometers)

Fun fact: Gypsum sand doesn't absorb heat the way that normal sand does, so the sand on these dunes won't scald your feet if you walk on them barefoot.

Photo op: Capture the beautiful dunes with a yucca in the foreground, which is especially beautiful at sunset.

Date of visit: _____

Weather/Temperature: ☀ ☁ ⛅ 🌧 ❄ 🌬 🌡🌡

Companions: _____

_____

_____

Favorite experiences: _____

_____

_____

_____

_____

_____

_____

_____

NEW MEXICO

Notable plants and wildlife:

Plan to return?   Yes   No

Notes for next visit:

Space for sketches and/or stamps:

Theodore Roosevelt National Park

EST. APRIL 1947

Although most commonly visited for its badlands, there's much more to see, including a large population of bison, fossils (including petrified wood), and unique, cannonball-shaped rock formations.

☐ THEODORE ROOSEVELT NATIONAL PARK

Size of park: 110 square miles (285 square kilometers)

Fun fact: The park is named for the twenty-sixth U.S. president, Theodore Roosevelt, who spent formative years of his life in this area. In fact, the park contains the land of a ranch he owned and his Maltese Cross Cabin.

Photo op: Boicourt Overlook Trail is a short trail with an epic payoff for some photos of the badlands.

Date of visit: ....

Weather/Temperature: ☀ ☁ ⛅ 🌧 🌨 💨 🌡🌡

Companions: ....

....

....

Favorite experiences: ....

....

....

....

....

....

....

....

Notable plants and wildlife:

_____

_____

_____

_____

Plan to return?   Yes   No

Notes for next visit: _____

_____

_____

_____

Space for sketches and/or stamps:

Cuyahoga Valley National Park

EST. JUNE 1975

This park highlights the beauty surrounding the snaking Cuyahoga River. Rolling hills, waterfalls, rock formations, and cultural sites all beckon you to take a step back into an Ohio of the past.

☐ CUYAHOGA VALLEY NATIONAL PARK

Size of park: 51 square miles (132 square kilometers)

Fun fact: The name Cuyahoga, which means "crooked river," comes from local Indigenous languages.

Photo op: Snap a pic from the observation deck at Brandywine Falls.

Date of visit:

Weather/Temperature:

Companions:

Favorite experiences:

OHIO

Notable plants and wildlife:

_____

_____

_____

_____

Plan to return?   Yes   No

Notes for next visit: _____

_____

_____

_____

_____

Space for sketches and/or stamps:

OHIO

Crater Lake National Park

EST. MAY 1902

Nestled in the Cascade Mountains, this park's vivid, deep blue lake formed inside a collapsed volcano. Although the lake is its big draw, there are waterfalls, overlooks, and lush forests as well.

☐ CRATER LAKE NATIONAL PARK

Size of park: 286 square miles (741 square kilometers)

Fun fact: Crater Lake is so deep that you could stack the Eiffel Tower, Statue of Liberty, and Washington Monument, and they wouldn't touch the surface of the lake.

Photo op: Watchman Peak shows off the most spectacular view of Crater Lake and Wizard Island.

Date of visit: ....

Weather/Temperature: ☀ ☁ ⛅ 🌧 🌨 🌬 🌡🌡

Companions: ....

....

....

Favorite experiences: ....

....

....

....

....

....

....

....

OREGON

Notable plants and wildlife: _____
_____
_____
_____
_____

Plan to return?   Yes   No

Notes for next visit: _____
_____
_____
_____
_____

Space for sketches and/or stamps:

Congaree National Park

EST. OCTOBER 1976

Congaree's trees are what this park is most famous for, including a large concentration of old-growth bald cypress trees, which help make up one of the tallest, oldest canopies in the eastern United States.

☐ CONGAREE NATIONAL PARK

Size of park: 42 square miles (109 square kilometers)

Fun fact: Although it often looks swampy, Congaree isn't a swamp at all; it's a floodplain.

Photo op: The Boardwalk Loop offers the best photo ops of the old-growth trees.

Date of visit: _____

Weather/Temperature: ☀ ☁ ⛅ 🌧 ❄ 🌬 🌡 🌡

Companions: _____

_____

_____

Favorite experiences: _____

_____

_____

_____

_____

_____

_____

_____

Notable plants and wildlife:

Plan to return?   Yes   No

Notes for next visit:

Space for sketches and/or stamps:

Badlands National Park

EST. JANUARY 1939

The Badlands are a collection of grooved, towering formations that drop off into canyons rising from the surrounding plains. It's a maze of uniquely rugged beauty filled with ancient fossils.

☐ BADLANDS NATIONAL PARK

Size of park: 379 square miles (982 square kilometers)

Fun fact: This whole park used to be underwater, which is a big part of what created the formations known as badlands.

Photo op: Big Badlands Overlook is the perfect spot to get the scale of the park.

Date of visit: ....

Weather/Temperature: ☀ ☁ ⛅ 🌧 🌨 🌬 🌡 🌡

Companions: ....

....

....

Favorite experiences: ....

....

....

....

....

....

....

....

Notable plants and wildlife: ....
....
....
....
....

Plan to return?   Yes   No

Notes for next visit: ....
....
....
....
....

Space for sketches and/or stamps:

Wind Cave National Park

EST. JANUARY 1903

Wind Cave is a massive, unique cave that sits below a prairie. Guided tours take you inside to see distinctive formations like boxwork, frostwork, and cave popcorn.

☐ WIND CAVE NATIONAL PARK

Size of park: 53 square miles (137 square kilometers)

Fun fact: Although many caves are now part of the National Park Service, Wind Cave was the first cave to be designated a national park in the world.

Photo op: Snap a pic of the boxwork inside Wind Cave, which looks like stone spiderwebs; they're found all over the cave and are unlike any other in the world.

Date of visit: ....

Weather/Temperature: ☀ ☁ ⛅ 🌧 ❄ 🌬 🌡

Companions: ....

....

....

Favorite experiences: ....

....

....

....

....

....

....

....

Notable plants and wildlife: _____

_____

_____

_____

_____

Plan to return?   Yes   No

Notes for next visit: _____

_____

_____

_____

_____

Space for sketches and/or stamps:

GREAT SMOKEY MOUNTIANS

• NATIONAL PARK •

Great Smoky Mountains National Park

EST. MAY 1926

Layer after layer of mountains as far as the eye can see, lush forests, waterfalls, wildflowers, streams, and an abundance of wildlife make this park unforgettable.

☐ GREAT SMOKY MOUNTAINS NATIONAL PARK

Size of park: 816 square miles (2,113 square kilometers)

Fun fact: The Great Smoky Mountains are known as the "Salamander Capital of the World." Thirty species of these amphibians live here.

Photo op: Newfound Gap offers some of the best views for a pic of the layers of the mountains.

Date of visit: _____

Weather/Temperature: ☀ ☁ ⛅ 🌧 ❄ 🌬 🌡 🌡

Companions: _____

_____

_____

Favorite experiences: _____

_____

_____

_____

_____

_____

_____

_____

_____

_____

Notable plants and wildlife:

_____

_____

_____

_____

Plan to return?   Yes   No

Notes for next visit: _____

_____

_____

_____

_____

Space for sketches and/or stamps:

Big Bend National Park

EST. JUNE 1935

Located in remote West Texas, this park combines many unique and beautiful elements: the Rio Grande, the Chisos Mountain range, canyons, rock formations, historical sites, and a natural hot spring!

☐ BIG BEND NATIONAL PARK

Size of park: 1,252 square miles (3,243 square kilometers)

Fun fact: Love stargazing? Big Bend has the darkest skies in the Lower 48!

Photo op: Take a pic looking back out of Santa Elena Canyon with the Chisos Mountains in the background.

Date of visit: _____

Weather/Temperature: ☀ ☁ ⛅ 🌧 🌨 💨 🌡🌡

Companions: _____

_____

_____

Favorite experiences: _____

_____

_____

_____

_____

_____

_____

_____

_____

Notable plants and wildlife: _____

_____

_____

_____

_____

Plan to return?   Yes   No

Notes for next visit: _____

_____

_____

_____

_____

Space for sketches and/or stamps:

Guadalupe Mountains
National Park

EST. OCTOBER 1966

The tallest mountains in the state,
a canyon, sand dunes, and desert
make this a stunning park to visit,
but the massive portion of Permian
fossil reef makes it memorable.

☐ GUADALUPE MOUNTAINS NATIONAL PARK

Size of park: 135 square miles (350 square kilometers)

Fun fact: The mountain range in Guadalupe Mountains National Park is shared with Carlsbad Caverns National Park, just across the border in New Mexico.

Photo op: Take a pic from the "Top of Texas"; Guadalupe Mountain is the highest peak in the state.

Date of visit: ....

Weather/Temperature: ☀ ☁ ⛅ 🌧 🌨 🌬 🌡

Companions: ....

....

....

Favorite experiences: ....

....

....

....

....

....

....

....

TEXAS

Notable plants and wildlife: _____
_____
_____
_____
_____

Plan to return?   Yes   No

Notes for next visit: _____
_____
_____
_____
_____

Space for sketches and/or stamps:

Arches National Park

EST. APRIL 1929

Stepping into Arches is like stepping into another world. It's home to over 2,000 natural stone arches, including the iconic Delicate Arch, and many other wild formations across its pink, orange, and red landscape.

☐ ARCHES NATIONAL PARK

Size of park: 120 square miles (310 square kilometers)

Fun fact: Arches is home to the highest concentration of natural arches in the world.

Photo op: Delicate Arch is worth the hike to see. It's arguably the most popular arch in the world.

Date of visit: _____

Weather/Temperature: ☀ ☁ ⛅ 🌦 🌨 💨 🌡🌡

Companions: _____

_____

_____

Favorite experiences: _____

_____

_____

_____

_____

_____

_____

_____

Notable plants and wildlife:

Plan to return?   Yes   No

Notes for next visit:

UTAH

Space for sketches and/or stamps:

Bryce Canyon National Park

EST. JUNE 1923

Bryce Canyon is a red rock wonderland. Most famous for its high concentration of funky hoodoo formations, there are several trails that bring you up close to these tall, totem pole–like rock formations and also offer spectacular vistas of the amphitheaters.

☐ BRYCE CANYON NATIONAL PARK

Size of park: 56 square miles (145 square kilometers)

Fun fact: Bryce Canyon isn't a canyon at all. It's actually a series of natural amphitheaters.

Photo op: Sunrise Point offers some of the best views of all the hoodoos in the park.

Date of visit: _____

Weather/Temperature: ☀ ☁ ⛅ 🌧 🌨 🌬 🌡 🌡

Companions: _____

_____

_____

Favorite experiences: _____

_____

_____

_____

_____

_____

_____

_____

_____

UTAH

Notable plants and wildlife: ....

....

....

....

....

Plan to return?   Yes   No

Notes for next visit: ....

....

....

....

....

Space for sketches and/or stamps:

UTAH

Canyonlands National Park

EST. SEPTEMBER 1964

Three sections (Island in the Sky, the Maze, and the Needles) make up this park. Deep canyons, shallower canyons, rivers, rock formations, and petroglyphs contribute to the beauty held within this park.

☐ CANYONLANDS NATIONAL PARK

Size of park: 527 square miles (1,365 square kilometers)

Fun fact: The Colorado and Green Rivers are sometimes considered the fourth district of the national park.

Photo op: Taking a pic of sunrise at Mesa Arch is crowded and popular for good reason.

Date of visit: _____

Weather/Temperature: ☀️ ⛅ 🌤️ 🌧️ 🌨️ 🌬️ 🌡️ 🌡️

Companions: _____

_____

_____

Favorite experiences: _____

_____

_____

_____

_____

_____

_____

_____

Notable plants and wildlife:

_____

_____

_____

_____

Plan to return?   Yes   No

Notes for next visit: _____

_____

_____

_____

_____

Space for sketches and/or stamps:

Capitol Reef National Park

EST. AUGUST 1937

Capitol Reef is known for its white dome formations (resembling capitol buildings). Natural bridges, canyons, other distinctive formations, and various petroglyphs across a red rock landscape set this park apart.

☐ CAPITOL REEF NATIONAL PARK

Size of park: 378 square miles (979 square kilometers)

Fun fact: Infamous Wild West criminal Butch Cassidy sought refuge in Capitol Reef.

Photo op: Catch the perfect shot of the massive monoliths in Cathedral Valley.

Date of visit: ....

Weather/Temperature: ☼ ☁ ⛅ ☔ ❄ 🌬 🌡 🌡

Companions: ....

....

....

Favorite experiences: ....

....

....

....

....

....

....

....

....

UTAH

Notable plants and wildlife:

_____

_____

_____

_____

Plan to return?   Yes   No

Notes for next visit: _____

_____

_____

_____

_____

Space for sketches and/or stamps:

ZION
· NATIONAL PARK ·

Zion National Park

EST. JULY 1909

The Virgin River carved out the steep but narrow red, orange, and pink walls of Zion Canyon to create some of the most beautiful sites and adventurous trails in the Southwest.

☐ ZION NATIONAL PARK

Size of park: 230 square miles (596 square kilometers)

Fun fact: Kolob Arch is the second longest known arch in the world. Landscape Arch in Arches National Park (page 158) is the longest.

Photo op: The view from Observation Point makes for one of the best photos of Zion Canyon. It even looks down on the famous Angels Landing.

Date of visit: _____

Weather/Temperature: ☀ ☁ ⛅ 🌧 🌨 🌬 🌡🌡

Companions: _____

_____

_____

Favorite experiences: _____

_____

_____

_____

_____

_____

_____

_____

UTAH

Notable plants and wildlife:

_____

_____

_____

_____

Plan to return?   Yes   No

Notes for next visit: _____

_____

_____

_____

_____

Space for sketches and/or stamps:

UTAH

Virgin Islands National Park

EST. AUGUST 1956

This park is more than pristine beaches and tropical forests. It holds thousands of years of history, such as Indigenous petroglyphs and Dutch plantation sites. Plus, snorkelers will love the reefs and wildlife here.

☐ VIRGIN ISLANDS NATIONAL PARK

Size of park: 24 square miles (62 square kilometers)

Fun fact: This park has an underwater snorkel trail that shows off and identifies the different corals located here.

Photo op: There is a stunning viewpoint of the island valley leading out to the ocean on the Reef Bay Trail.

Date of visit: ....

Weather/Temperature: ☀ ☁ ⛅ 🌧 ❄ 🌬 🌡 🌡

Companions: ....

....

....

Favorite experiences: ....

....

....

....

....

....

....

....

Notable plants and wildlife: _____
_____
_____
_____
_____

Plan to return?   Yes   No

Notes for next visit: _____
_____
_____
_____
_____

Space for sketches and/or stamps:

Shenandoah National Park

EST. MAY 1926

Situated in the Blue Ridge Mountains, this park has spectacular views, especially from certain trails and Skyline Drive. Densely forested paths lead to stunning waterfalls and craggy overlooks.

☐ SHENANDOAH NATIONAL PARK

Size of park: 313 square miles (811 square kilometers)

Fun fact: The Appalachian Trail, the famous mountain hike that goes from Georgia to Maine, cuts through Shenandoah National Park; 101 miles (almost 5 percent) of it are within the park!

Photo op: The Point Overlook, located just off Skyline Drive, is a perfect spot to see all the layers of mountains, especially for a sunset photo.

Date of visit: _____

Weather/Temperature: ☀ ☁ ⛅ 🌦 🌨 🌬 🌡🌡

Companions: _____

_____

_____

Favorite experiences: _____

_____

_____

_____

_____

_____

_____

_____

VIRGINIA

Notable plants and wildlife: _____

_____

_____

_____

_____

Plan to return? Yes No

Notes for next visit: _____

_____

_____

_____

_____

Space for sketches and/or stamps:

Mount Rainier National Park

EST. MARCH 1899

Mount Rainier is a massive active volcano covered with twenty-five glaciers. The park boasts mountains, valleys covered with summertime blooms, and the only inland rainforest.

☐ MOUNT RAINIER NATIONAL PARK

Size of park: 369 square miles (956 square kilometers)

Fun fact: This park is famous for the hundreds of different wildflower species that bloom in spring and summer.

Photo op: Capture the perfect photo of Mount Rainier with Myrtle Falls in the foreground, which is found on the Skyline Trail.

Date of visit: _____

Weather/Temperature: ☼ ☁ ⛅ 🌧 🌨 💨 🌡 🌡

Companions: _____

_____

_____

Favorite experiences: _____

_____

_____

_____

_____

_____

_____

_____

WASHINGTON

Notable plants and wildlife: _____

_____

_____

_____

_____

Plan to return?   Yes   No

Notes for next visit: _____

_____

_____

_____

_____

Space for sketches and/or stamps:

North Cascades National Park

EST. OCTOBER 1968

This park is a mountain lovers paradise. It's filled with mountains covered in glaciers, brightly colored lakes, waterfalls, and old-growth forests filled with firs, ferns, fungi, and wildlife.

☐ NORTH CASCADES NATIONAL PARK

Size of park: 789 square miles (2,043 square kilometers)

Fun fact: With over 300 glaciers, North Cascades has more glaciers than any other national park in the Lower 48.

Photo op: Picture Lake offers great photo opportunities any time of day. You can capture Mount Shuksan's reflection with blue skies, colorful skies at sunset, or starry skies at night.

Date of visit: _____

Weather/Temperature: ☀ ☁ ⛅ 🌧 ❄ 💨 🌡🌡

Companions: _____

_____

_____

Favorite experiences: _____

_____

_____

_____

_____

_____

_____

_____

Notable plants and wildlife:

_____

_____

_____

_____

Plan to return?   Yes   No

Notes for next visit: _____

_____

_____

_____

_____

Space for sketches and/or stamps:

WASHINGTON

Olympic National Park

EST. MARCH 1909

Olympic feels like multiple parks in one. The snowcapped Olympic Mountains stand tall over the other sections. The rainforest is unbelievably green. The rugged, rocky coastal areas have sea stacks, tide pools, and other natural formations.

☐ OLYMPIC NATIONAL PARK

Size of park: 1,442 square miles (3,735 square kilometers)

Fun fact: You can actually see gray whales from certain beaches during migration season.

Photo op: The view from the top of Hurricane Ridge is one of the most stunning photographs you can take in this park.

Date of visit: ....

Weather/Temperature: ☀ ☁ 🌤 🌧 🌨 🌬 🌡🌡

Companions: ....

....

....

Favorite experiences: ....

....

....

....

....

....

....

....

Notable plants and wildlife: _____

_____

_____

_____

_____

Plan to return?   Yes   No

Notes for next visit: _____

_____

_____

_____

Space for sketches and/or stamps:

New River Gorge National Park and Preserve

EST. NOVEMBER 1978

The New River carved a deep gorge out of the Appalachians. Whitewater rafters love getting on the powerful river, and hikers will be thrilled with the trails throughout the surrounding forest.

☐ NEW RIVER GORGE NATIONAL PARK AND PRESERVE

Size of park: 113 square miles (293 square kilometers)

Fun fact: Despite its name, New River is actually one of the oldest rivers in the world.

Photo op: Photograph the New River Gorge Bridge from the Canyon Rim Visitor Center, which has a perfect overlook.

Date of visit: ....

Weather/Temperature: ☀ ☁ ⛅ 🌧 🌨 🌬 🌡

Companions: ....

....

....

Favorite experiences: ....

....

....

....

....

....

....

Notable plants and wildlife: _____
_____
_____
_____
_____

Plan to return?   Yes   No

Notes for next visit: _____
_____
_____
_____
_____

Space for sketches and/or stamps:

Grand Teton National Park

EST. FEBRUARY 1929

The Teton Mountains are the park's crown jewels, but they're only the beginning. The Teton Range is forty miles long. The park also contains waterfalls, six glacial lakes, and tons of wildlife.

☐ GRAND TETON NATIONAL PARK

Size of park: 484 square miles (1,254 square kilometers)

Fun fact: These are the youngest mountains in the Rocky Mountain chain, and they're actually still growing!

Photo op: Get that perfect reflection pic of the Tetons at Jenny Lake.

Date of visit: ....

Weather/Temperature: ☀️ ☁️ 🌤️ 🌧️ 🌨️ 🌬️ 🌡️ 🌡️

Companions: ....

....

....

Favorite experiences: ....

....

....

....

....

....

....

....

....

Notable plants and wildlife: ....
....
....
....
....

Plan to return?   Yes   No

Notes for next visit: ....
....
....
....
....

Space for sketches and/or stamps:

Yellowstone National Park

EST. MARCH 1872

Although the mountains, waterfalls, and lakes here
are stunning, Yellowstone is most famous for its
wide array of geothermal features, such as geysers,
multicolored pools, hot springs, and mud pots.

☐ YELLOWSTONE NATIONAL PARK

Size of park: 3,468 square miles (8,982 square kilometers)

Fun fact: Yellowstone sits atop a massive super volcano, so it's no surprise that there are over 10,000 hydrothermal features inside the park.

Photo op: Capture the iconic Grand Prismatic Spring from the overlook of the same name. It's a short hike but worth it to get to see the wide array of colors from above the steam.

Date of visit: _____

Weather/Temperature: ☀ ☁ ⛅ 🌧 ❄ 🌬 🌡🌡

Companions: _____

_____

_____

Favorite experiences: _____

_____

_____

_____

_____

_____

_____

_____

_____

Notable plants and wildlife:

_____

_____

_____

_____

Plan to return?   Yes   No

Notes for next visit: _____

_____

_____

_____

_____

Space for sketches and/or stamps:

ACKNOWLEDGMENTS

I'd like to thank a few people who made this book possible. First of all, my parents, who instilled a love for the U.S. national parks. Secondly, my husband, Matt, who shares a love of the parks and always supports my crazy ideas. We can't wait to fill this logbook along with our daughter, Charleigh, and son, Liam. I love you all immensely. Also, thank you to everyone who helps maintain these public lands for all the generations to come.

ABOUT THE AUTHOR

Paige Wunder is a proud mother, wife and the creator and writer of the travel blog *For the Love of Wanderlust*, detailing her adventures across all 50 states and dozens of countries. Her passions are exploring the outdoors, experiencing different cultures, fostering a love for nature in her little ones, and attempting to live a more sustainable life. When she isn't traveling she's hiking, crocheting, or playing at home with her husband and their two children in the heart of the Ozarks.